I LOVE YOU

BECAUSE

MARIANNE RICHMOND

Published by Sourcebooks, Inc.
P.O. Box 4410, Naperville, Illinois 60567-4410
(630) 961-3900
Fax: (630) 961-2168
www.sourcebooks.com

Printed and bound in China.

LEO 10 9 8 7 6 5 4 3 2 1

3178 0743

To: _____

From: _____

I love you because

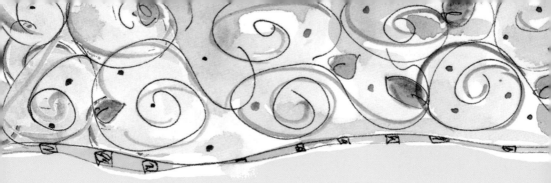

you're you.

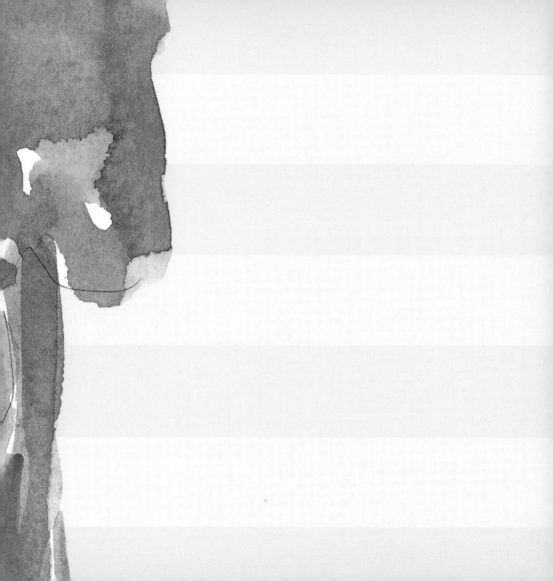

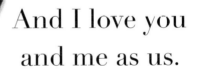

And I love you
and me as us.

I'm so grateful that our paths crossed along the way.

And I'm grateful that
we share the same crazy
affection for one another.

I can't imagine life
without you.

I love you for accepting the
various versions of me...

Silly me

Questioning me

Whiny me

Happy me

Irrational (ok, I admit it) me.

I love you for accepting that
the "drives-you-crazy" me
is just one itty-bitty part of
the greater, lovable me.

I love you for the way you make
"everyday-ness" more fun.

Our routines

Our inside jokes

Our adventures

I love you because
you make me laugh.

And you think I'm funny, too.
(You do, don't you?)

I love you for
encouraging me when

I'm not feeling very brave
or capable or successful.

You help me see the positive,
and I need that.

I love you for trying to accept my need for "me time" and my bad habits.

I love you for trying to understand my ways,

even when you can't possibly
understand my ways.

I love you for saying you like
the change to my hair,

even if you can't really notice
the change to my hair.

I love you for your smile.

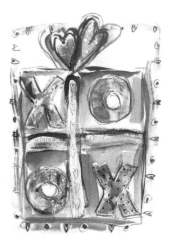

I love you for your laughter,
hugs, and kisses, too.

I

love, love, love
each and
every inch
of you!

I love cuddling with you.

I love you for making important
to you what's important to me.

I know we don't *always* agree.
I love that we can voice our opinions,
even get mad at each other, and we
still love each other through it.

I love being able
to coexist with you
in the same quiet space,

knowing we don't have to talk to enjoy one another.

I love you because you
stretch yourself to become
a better person.

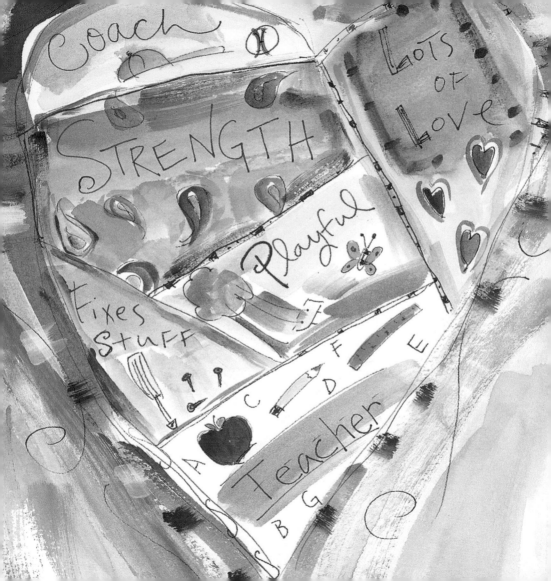

To learn more
and to love more.

I love creating

the story of our love.

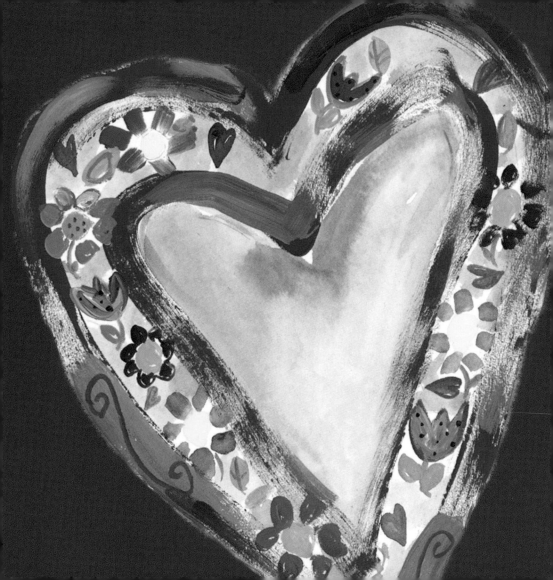

I love that we have a history,
memories, dreams, and
genuine concern for the
daily-ness of each other's lives.

I love the thought of journeying through this crazy world together, wherever it takes us.

I love you because you're my
life mate and my soul mate.

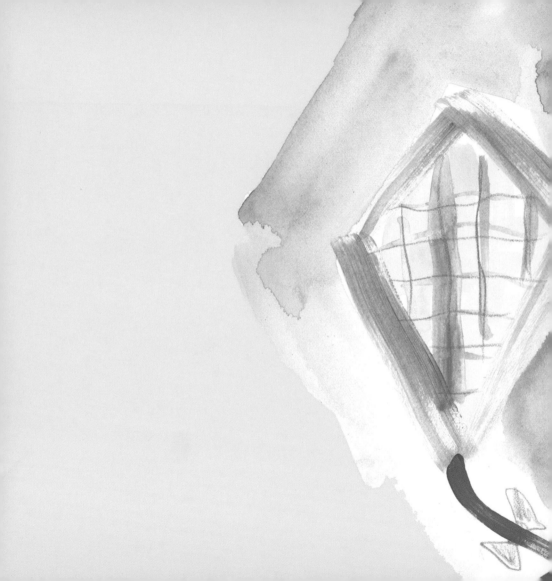

You're my best friend.

I love you because you're
my everything.

And my one and only.

About the Author

Beloved author and artist Marianne Richmond has touched the lives of millions for nearly two decades through her award-winning books, greeting cards, and other gift products that offer people the most heartfelt way to connect with each other. She lives in the Minneapolis area. Visit www.mariannerichmond.com.